SMART ONLINE RESEARCH

THE INTERNET SAFETY HANDBOOK

INVESTIGATE!

BY CHARLEY LIGHT

Enslow PUBLISHING

Please visit our website, www.enslow.com. For a free color catalog of all our high-quality books, call toll free 1-800-398-2504 or fax 1-877-980-4454.

Cataloging-in-Publication Data

Names: Light, Charley.
Title: Smart online research / Charley Light.
Description: New York : Enslow Publishing, 2024. | Series: The internet safety handbook | Includes glossary and index.
Identifiers: ISBN 9781978535039 (pbk.) | ISBN 9781978535046 (library bound) | ISBN 9781978535053 (ebook)
Subjects: LCSH: Cyberspace–Juvenile literature. | Electronic information resources–Juvenile literature. | Research–Methodology–Juvenile literature.
Classification: LCC ZA4060.L54 2024 | DDC 025.04–dc23

Published in 2024 by
Enslow Publishing
2544 Clinton Street
Buffalo, NY 14224

Copyright © 2024 Enslow Publishing

Portions of this work were originally authored by Barbara M. Linde and published as *Cyberspace Research*. All new material in this edition authored by Charley Light.

Designer: Jen Schoembs
Editor: Charley Light

Photo credits: Cover (Boy), p. 1 (boy) Eton White/Shutterstock.com; cover (background), p. 1, series art (background) kerly chonglor/Shutterstock.com; p. 5 Panya_photo/Shutterstock.com; p. 7 Kumar Sriskandan/Alamy.com; pp. 9, 11 Ground Picture/Shutterstock.com; p. 11 Ground Picture/Shutterstock.com; p. 13 Wachiwit/Shutterstock.com; p. 15 Evelyn D. Harrison/Shutterstock.com; pp. 17, 29 Prostock-studio/Shutterstock.com; p. 19 Nedrofly/Shutterstock.com; p. 23 Funstock/Shutterstock.com; p. 25 kali9/iStock.com.

All rights reserved. No part of this book may be reproduced in any form without permission in writing from the publisher, except by a reviewer.

Some of the images in this book illustrate individuals who are models. The depictions do not imply actual situations or events.

Printed in the United States of America

CPSIA compliance information: Batch #CSENS24: For further information contact Enslow Publishing at 1-800-398-2504.

Find us on

CONTENTS

Research Detective 4
Sources 6
Where Are We Going? 8
Know Your Tools 10
Browsing for Browsers 12
Keywords 14
Sus Sources 16
As a Matter of Fact... 18
What's In a (Domain) Name? 20
Says Who? 24
Cite Your Sources 26
The Investigation Is Never Done 28
Glossary 30
For More Information 31
Index 32

Words in the glossary appear in **bold** type the first time they are used in the text.

RESEARCH DETECTIVE

Have you ever seen a detective story? The detective goes on an **investigation** for information. They talk to different people, called sources, to get the scoop. When they have gathered all the facts, they can solve the mystery.

Research is a chance for you to put on a detective cap of your own and seek out facts! You can find lots of different sources online. Sometimes it can be tricky to tell the difference between fact and fiction. This book will help you **sleuth** your way to the truth!

EXPLORE MORE

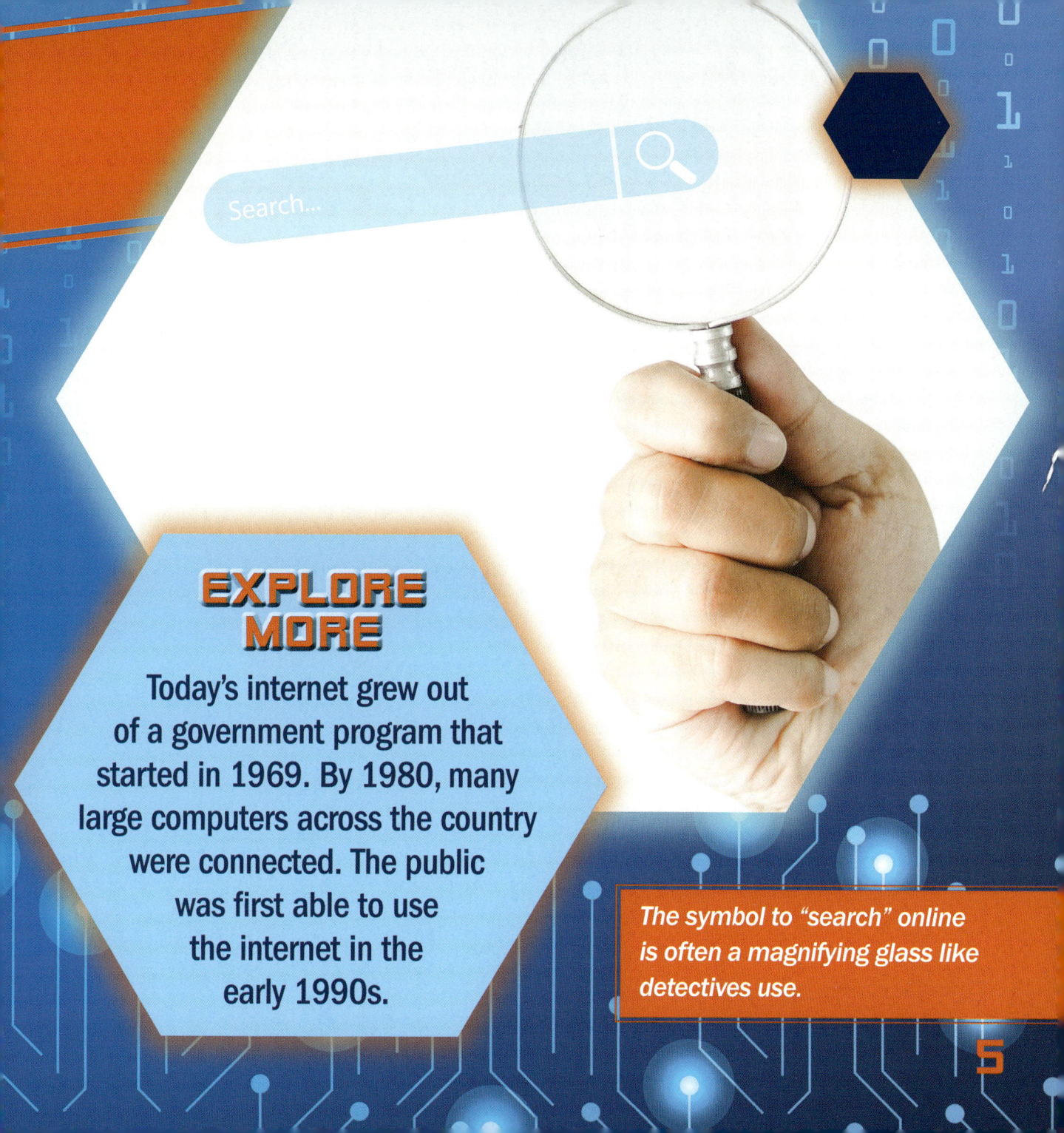

Today's internet grew out of a government program that started in 1969. By 1980, many large computers across the country were connected. The public was first able to use the internet in the early 1990s.

The symbol to "search" online is often a magnifying glass like detectives use.

SOURCES

Detectives talk to different sources to hear their side of a story. Each source helps the detective put together the whole story. When you look for sources of information online, you're also piecing together facts from different places to get a bigger picture about the topic you're researching.

You'll find two main types of sources in your research. Primary sources are original pieces of information—such as the Declaration of Independence. Secondary sources are things that talk about original information. A website about the Declaration of Independence is a secondary source.

EXPLORE MORE

Some sources online, such as *Encyclopedia Britannica*, cost money. You can get some information there for free, but there's a fee to use the whole site. The fee may be worth it if you plan to do a lot of research, because you know you can trust it as a source.

If you see the Declaration of Independence in person, you can use it as a primary source!

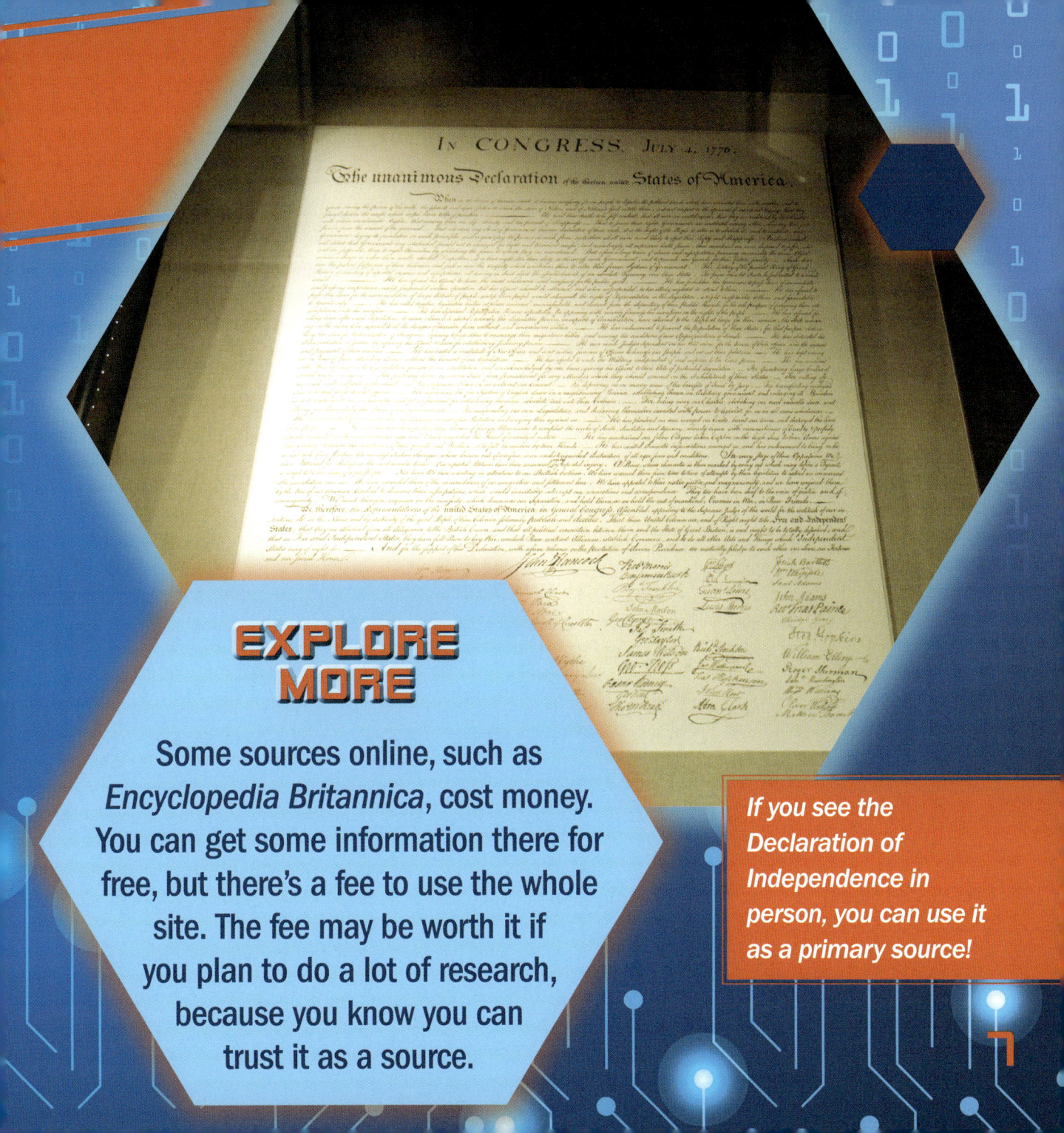

WHERE ARE WE GOING?

All detectives need tools to find the truth. The internet is a powerful tool for helping you conduct research. As with all tools, your results are most effective when you use it correctly. Following some basic guidelines will turn you into an intelligent internet investigator.

As you research, you'll be exploring the World Wide Web. That's the part of the internet where websites and their pages can be found. The web includes text, pictures, audio, and video content. This content will make up your sources.

EXPLORE MORE

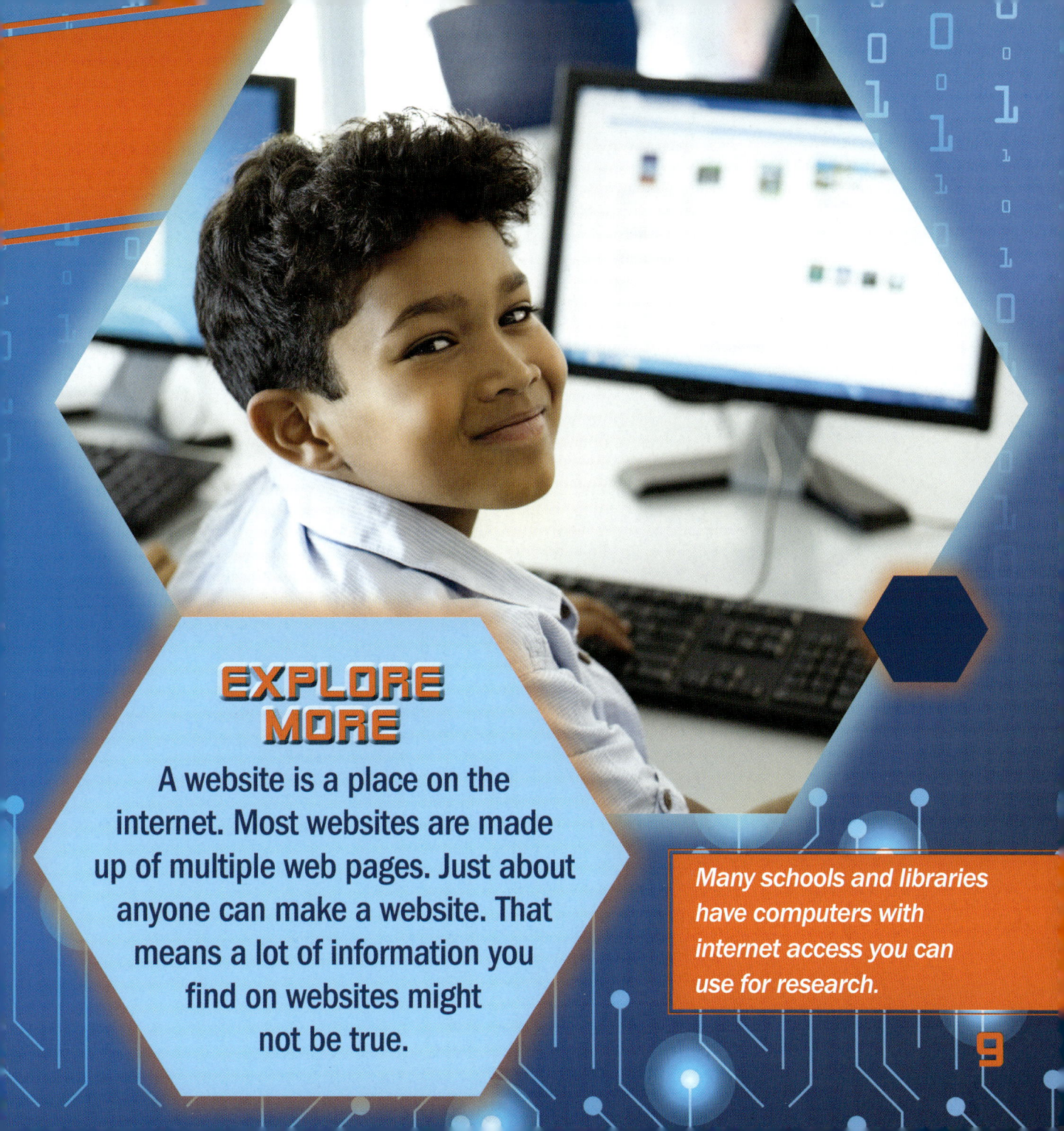

A website is a place on the internet. Most websites are made up of multiple web pages. Just about anyone can make a website. That means a lot of information you find on websites might not be true.

Many schools and libraries have computers with internet access you can use for research.

KNOW YOUR TOOLS

To search the web, you need a web browser. This is a program that allows access to the internet. Google Chrome, Mozilla Firefox, and Apple Safari are common browsers.

Once you're on a browser, you'll use a search engine to find sources. This is a program that searches the web using keywords. (You'll learn more about keywords on pages 14 and 15.) Google, Bing, and Yahoo! are common search engines. You can mix and match some web browsers and search engines. For example, the Mozilla Firefox web browser uses Google as its search engine.

EXPLORE MORE

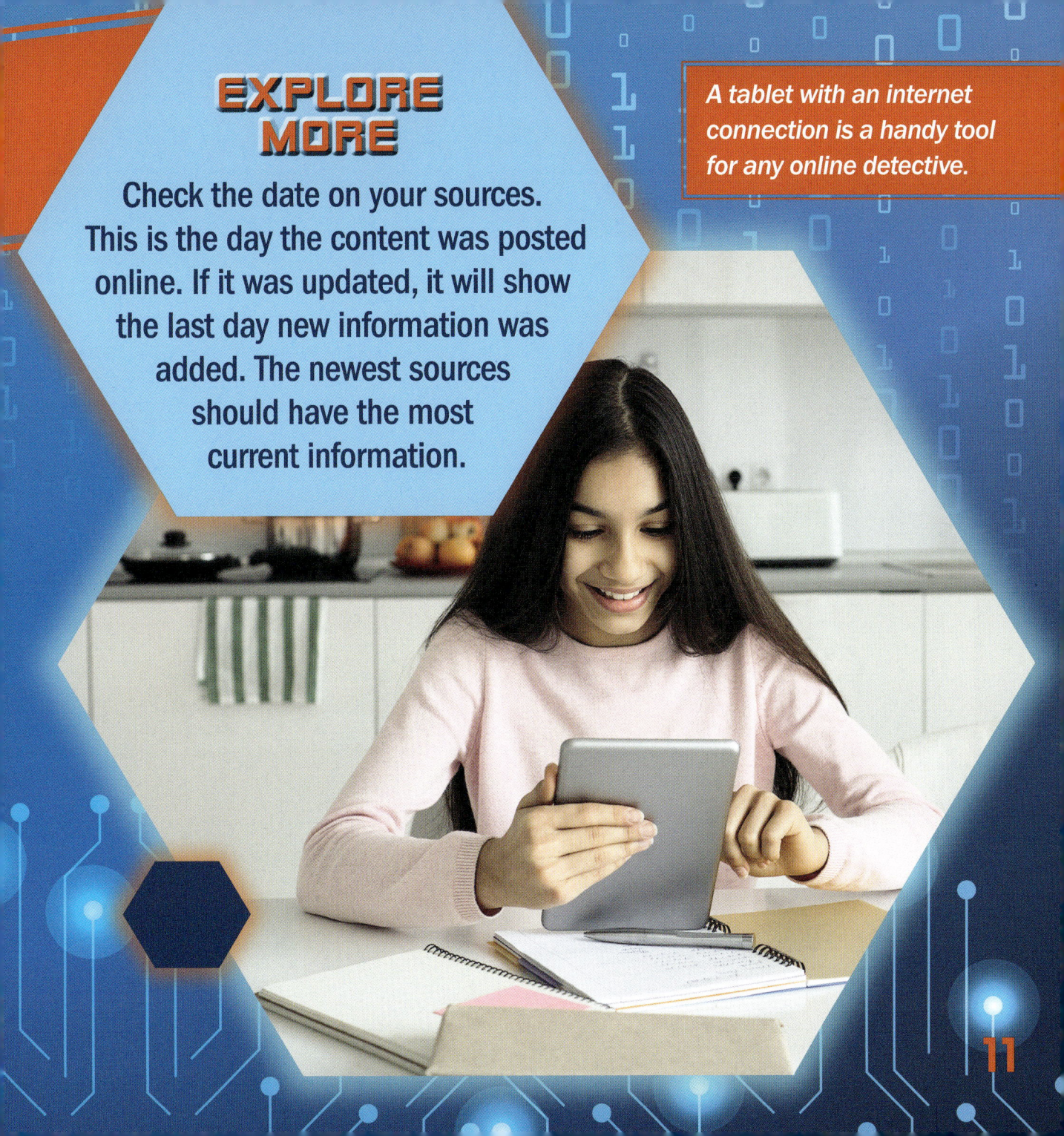

Check the date on your sources. This is the day the content was posted online. If it was updated, it will show the last day new information was added. The newest sources should have the most current information.

A tablet with an internet connection is a handy tool for any online detective.

BROWSING FOR BROWSERS

To open a browser, click the browser icon on your computer or smart device. This will take you to the browser's **home page**. There will be a search engine on the home page. It's also called a search bar. This is where you can begin looking for sources by entering a keyword! You'll learn more about this in the next chapter.

As you search, you can open multiple tabs on your browser. Each tab lets you go to a website. This way, you can have many sources open at once!

EXPLORE MORE

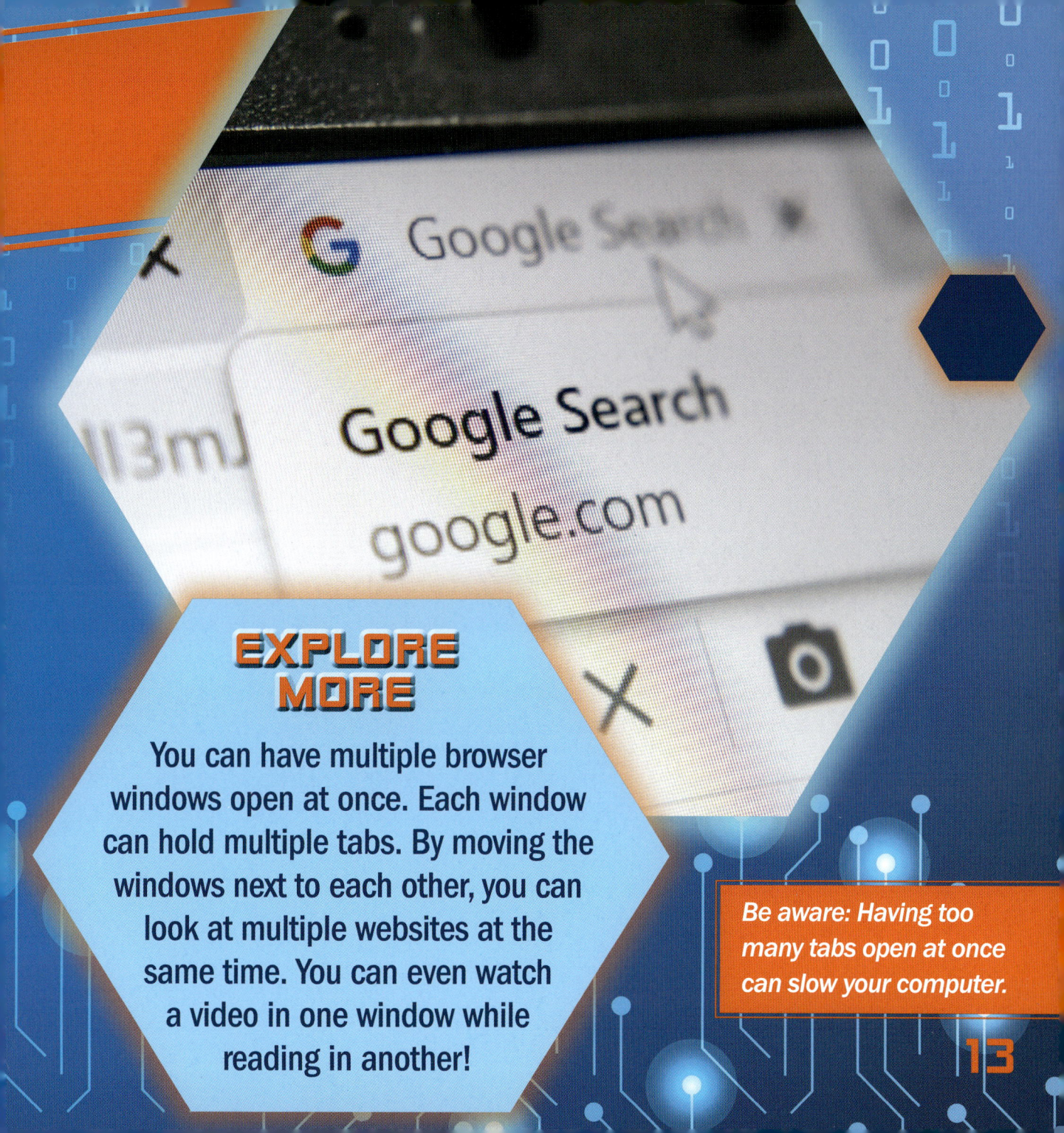

You can have multiple browser windows open at once. Each window can hold multiple tabs. By moving the windows next to each other, you can look at multiple websites at the same time. You can even watch a video in one window while reading in another!

Be aware: Having too many tabs open at once can slow your computer.

KEYWORDS

Keywords are terms that help the browser know what you're looking for. That way it can bring you the web pages that are most **relevant** to your quest.

Let's say you're researching coyotes. "Coyote" could be your first keyword! When you type it in and press search, lots of pages with the word "coyote" will pop up. Most will probably be about the animal. But some might not be helpful to you, such as a business with "Coyote" in its name. Time to get more **specific**!

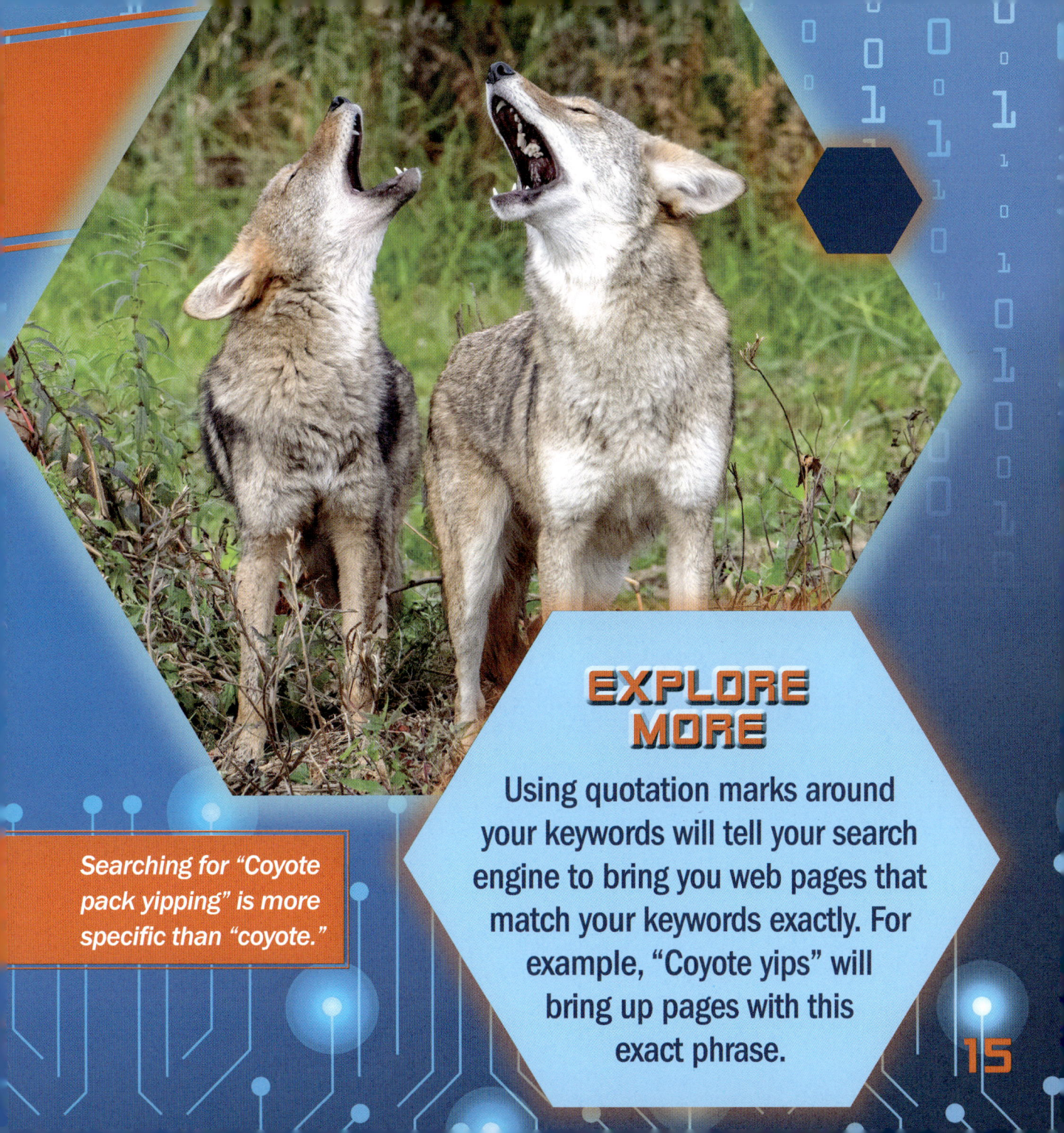

Searching for "Coyote pack yipping" is more specific than "coyote."

EXPLORE MORE

Using quotation marks around your keywords will tell your search engine to bring you web pages that match your keywords exactly. For example, "Coyote yips" will bring up pages with this exact phrase.

SUS SOURCES

In detective stories and on your web browser, sometimes sources don't tell the full truth. Websites, photographs, videos, and other content you find online can be misleading. This means they **misrepresent** true information to push you in the wrong direction.

Sources can also lie on purpose. Content makers online can make up statements that aren't true. People can also edit content to twist or hide the truth. Sometimes, sources online have incorrect information by accident. Some sources are simply **outdated**. Sometimes information changes over time as people learn more about a topic.

EXPLORE MORE

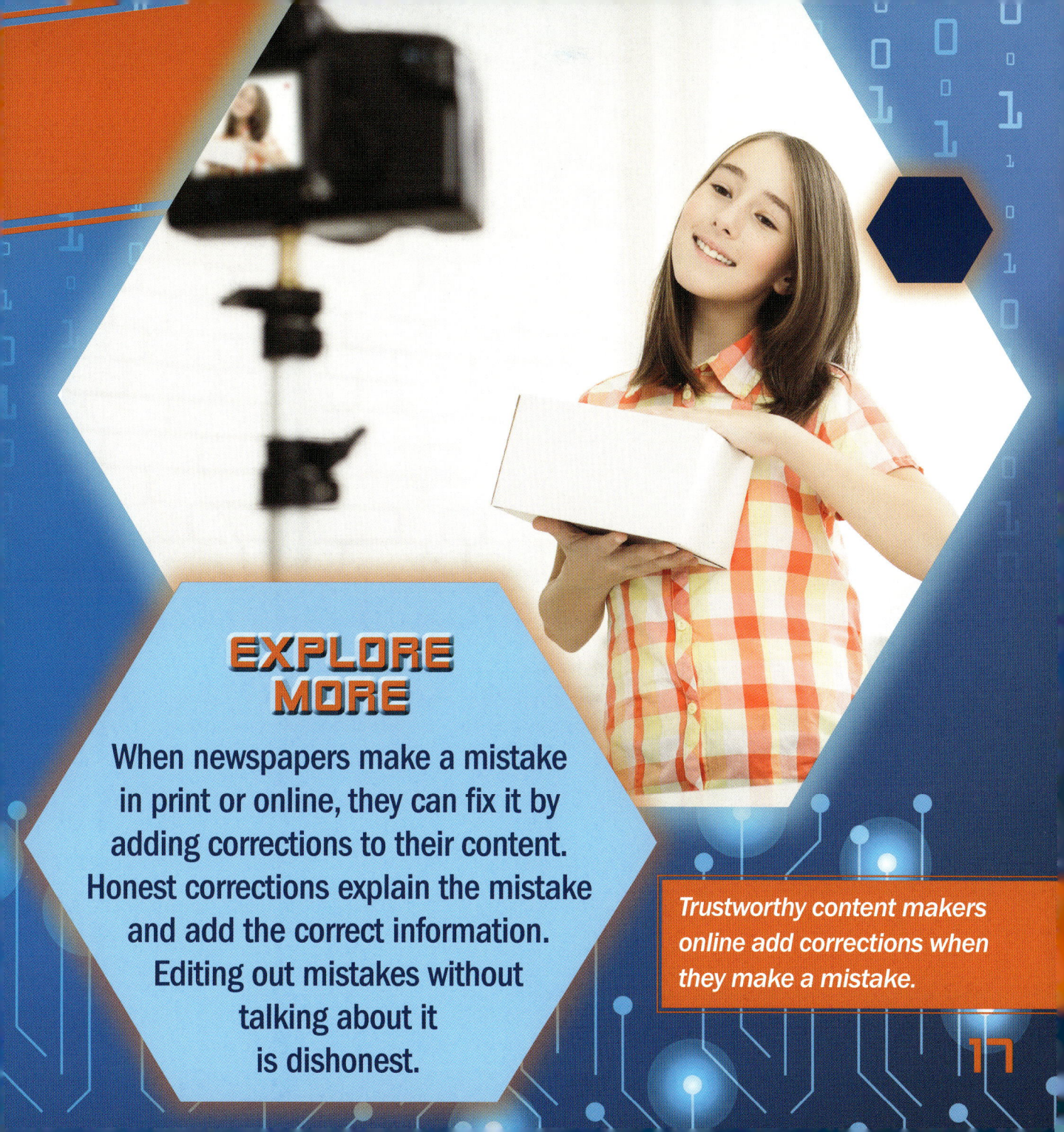

When newspapers make a mistake in print or online, they can fix it by adding corrections to their content. Honest corrections explain the mistake and add the correct information. Editing out mistakes without talking about it is dishonest.

Trustworthy content makers online add corrections when they make a mistake.

AS A MATTER OF FACT...

A good detective compares the stories of all the sources they talk to. This helps them see where the sources' stories don't match. This can sometimes mean one of the sources is lying or mistaken.

Comparing multiple sources on a topic you're researching helps you catch misrepresentation, lies, and mistakes in your sources. This is a process called fact-checking. When you find a fact in one source, you need to check other sources to see if their information matches. If multiple trustworthy sources online all have the same fact, it's probably true!

EXPLORE MORE

Facts are statements that can be proven true or false. *"Canis latrans* is the scientific name for coyotes" is a fact. Opinions are beliefs or feelings people hold about a topic. Opinions can't be proven true or false. "Coyotes are cool" is an opinion.

Take notes while you research. Include sources to make fact-checking easier!

WHAT'S IN A (DOMAIN) NAME?

How can you tell if your source is trustworthy? Like any good detective, you look for clues. The URL of a website gives you a lot of useful information. It has three main parts: a code, a domain name, and a domain extension.

The code is usually "http://" or "https://." It helps browsers read sites on the internet. The domain name is the address of the website. It tells other computers how to locate the information. The domain extension gives you a clue about where the information comes from.

EXPLORE MORE

URL stands for Uniform Resource Locator. It's the address for the website or online file. Every website has its own address, just like you have a street address. Typing a domain name into a browser is like typing a street address into a **GPS**.

Many URLs also include the name of the specific web page you are looking at on a website.

PARTS OF A URL

code — https://
domain extension — .com
domain name — www.funfacts
web page — cool-coyote-facts

https://www.funfacts.com/cool-coyote-facts

Remember that clue hiding inside a domain extension? It tells you what kind of source a website might be. Some common domain extensions in the United States are ".com," ".edu," ".gov," and ".org."

A ".com" domain can be used by just about anyone who makes a website, but sometimes it means **commerce.** A ".edu" is short for "education." This means it's probably a website made by an educational group like a school. A ".gov" shows you the source is a government website. A ".org" shows the website belongs to an organization.

EXPLORE MORE

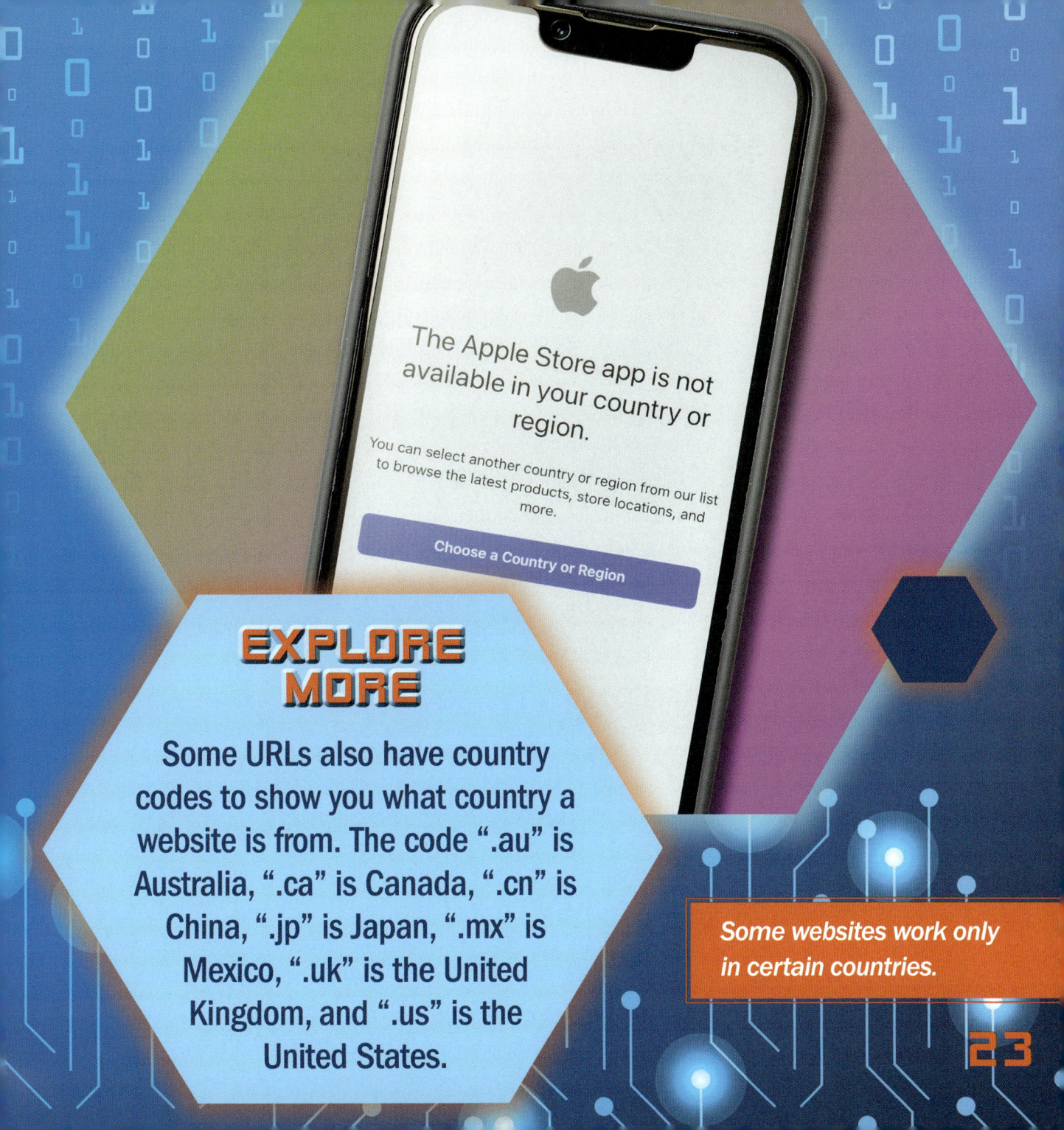

Some URLs also have country codes to show you what country a website is from. The code ".au" is Australia, ".ca" is Canada, ".cn" is China, ".jp" is Japan, ".mx" is Mexico, ".uk" is the United Kingdom, and ".us" is the United States.

Some websites work only in certain countries.

SAYS WHO?

Detectives need to know who is telling the story—and so do you! Look for the name of the creator. You can type the creator's name in your search engine to learn more about them. This can help you decide if you trust what they say in their content.

Many content creators also include a short **bio** right on the source. For example, the writer Penelope Fox's bio might tell you she has a degree in animal science, which means she went to college to learn about animals. This is a clue you can probably trust her "Cool Facts About Coyotes" article.

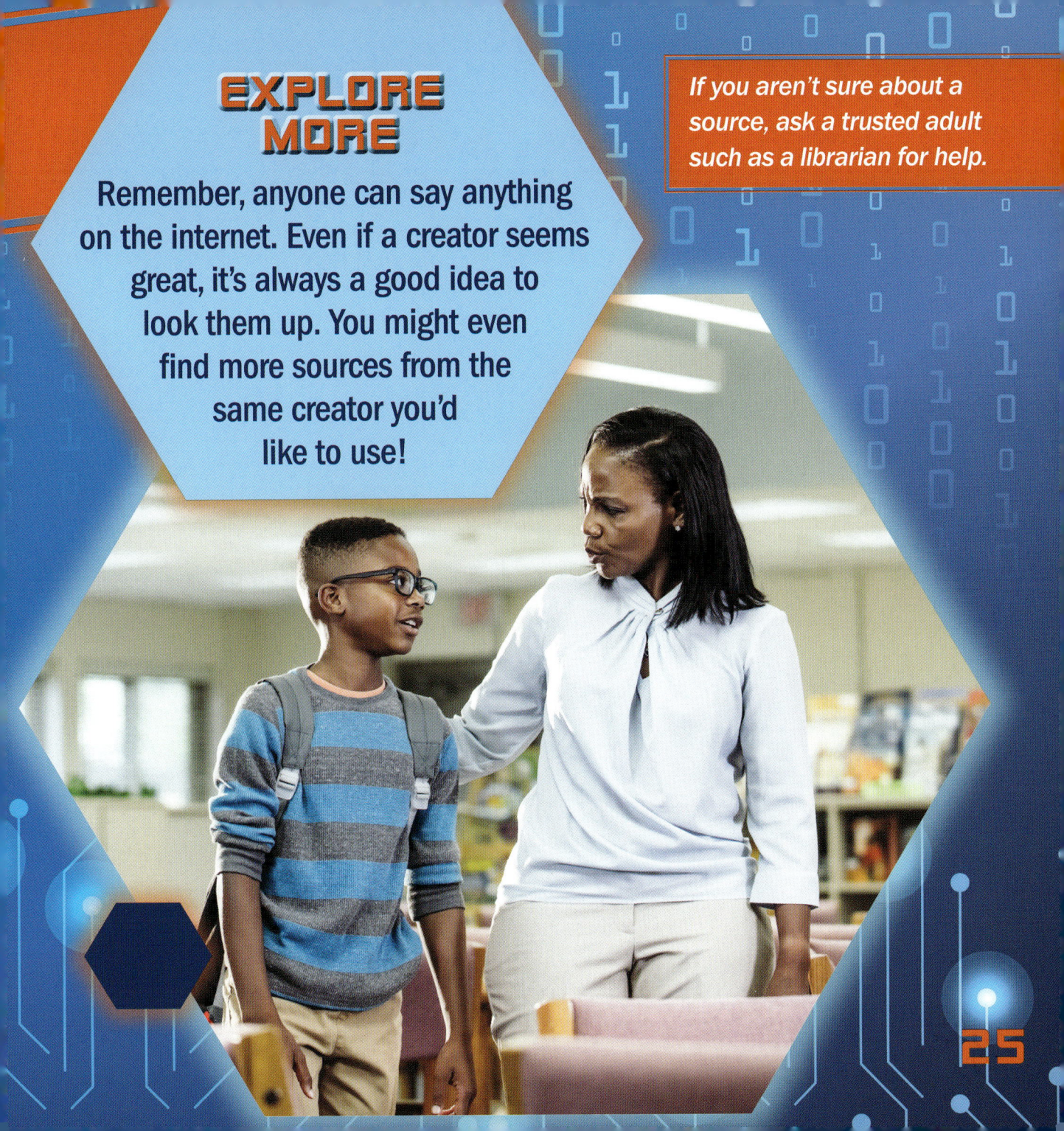

EXPLORE MORE

Remember, anyone can say anything on the internet. Even if a creator seems great, it's always a good idea to look them up. You might even find more sources from the same creator you'd like to use!

If you aren't sure about a source, ask a trusted adult such as a librarian for help.

CITE YOUR SOURCES

The detective writes down the names of all the sources they talk to. That way, they know who said what. And they can find each source again if they need to!

When you're researching online, you need to keep track of your sources too. This makes it easier to cite them later. Citing a source means giving proper credit to the place you found the information. Using information without giving proper credit is a kind of stealing called plagiarizing. Trustworthy sources of information will show you *their* sources too.

HOW TO CITE A WEB PAGE

author | title of the web page | website name

Fox, Penelope. "Cool Coyote Facts." FunFacts, www.funfacts.com/cool-coyote-facts. Accessed 1 March 2023.

link to the web page | day you read the source

There are different formats for citing sources. This one is in MLA format.

EXPLORE MORE

You can save a website for later by adding it to your "bookmarks." You can even organize your bookmarks into folders. This can help you visit websites again and again. Each web browser has its own bookmarking tools.

THE INVESTIGATION IS NEVER DONE

Any detective can tell you that the search for truth is never over. There's always another mystery to investigate! There are lots of educational videos for kids on YouTube. You can also find educational **podcasts** to listen to for free online. These are audio programs that come in episodes.

With a guardian's help, you can subscribe to YouTube channels and podcasts. This means you will get an alert when new content is released. Be sure to make a safety plan with a guardian for your internet investigation. You can even research together!

EXPLORE MORE

To take your internet investigation to the next level, try a search engine that is made for scholarly content. This is content made by researchers, teachers, and even other students. Google Scholar at https://scholar.google.com is a great place to start.

If you like to learn by listening, you can hear many free educational podcasts online.

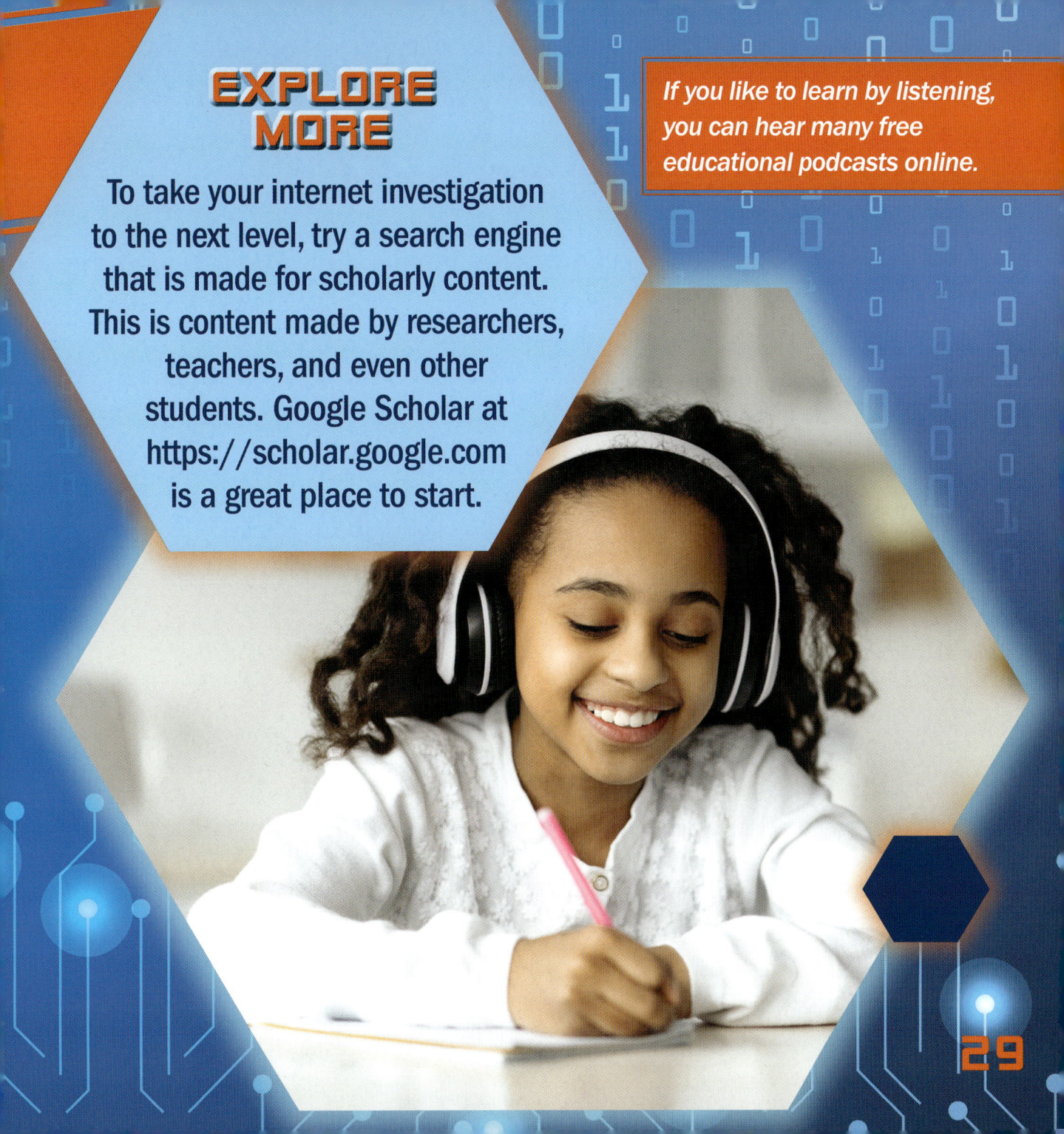

GLOSSARY

bio: A short description about someone.

commerce: The buying or selling of goods.

GPS: Global positioning system.

home page: The main page of a website.

investigation: A search for answers.

misrepresent: To give false information or twist the truth in order to trick someone.

outdated: No longer accurate.

podcasts: A program of music or talk available for download over the internet.

relevant: Related to a topic.

sleuth: Seeking truth.

specific: Detailed and precise.

FOR MORE INFORMATION

BOOKS

Giles, Sara. *Write Like a …: Creative Writing Activity Workbook for Curious and Creative Kids.* Seattle, WA: Birch Books, 2021.

Grant, Joyce and Kathleen Marcotte. *Can You Believe It?: How to Spot Fake News and Find the Facts.* Toronto, ON: Kids Can Press, 2022.

Rex, Michael. *Facts vs. Opinions vs. Robots.* New York, NY: Nancy Paulsen Books, 2020.

WEBSITES

DK Find Out
www.dkfindout.com/us
This site for kids has tons of cool facts on all kinds of topics!

Google Scholar
scholar.google.com
Find scholarly articles using this search engine!

Kiddle
www.kiddle.co
Kiddle is an educational search engine made just for kids!

Publisher's note to educators and parents: Our editors have carefully reviewed these websites to ensure that they are suitable for students. Many websites change frequently, however, and we cannot guarantee that a site's future contents will continue to meet our high standards of quality and educational value. Be advised that students should be closely supervised whenever they access the internet.

INDEX

Apple Safari, 10

Bing, 8

corrections, 17

Declaration of Independence, 6, 7

fact-checking, 18, 19

Google, 8

Google Chrome, 10

Google Scholar, 29

misrepresentation, 16, 18

Mozilla Firefox, 10

plagiarizing, 26

podcasts, 28, 29

primary sources, 6, 7

secondary sources, 6

Uniform Resource Locator, 21

World Wide Web, 8

Yahoo!, 8

YouTube, 28